Creation's Sensible Sequence

John B. Mulder

PUBLISH AMERICA

PublishAmerica
Baltimore

ISBN: 1-4241-5113-9
PUBLISHED BY PUBLISHAMERICA, LLLP
www.publishamerica.com
Baltimore

Printed in the United States of America

Dedication

This book is dedicated to my dear wife, Wilma Deane, who for fifty years has encouraged me, edited my many manuscripts, cared well for our family, and always remained my trusted best friend.

Manuscript Review

Grammatical review and editing of this manuscript were provided by Wilma D. Mulder, BS, English and Literature, former high school teacher.

Author's Website

www.jmulder.org

Contents

Introduction

"Thus says the Lord who made the Earth, the Lord who formed it to establish it—the Lord is his name. Call to me and I will answer you, and will tell you great and hidden things that you have not known" (Jeremiah 33:2-3).

The thrust of this book is to show God's divine strategy in ensuring sensible, exacting sequences during his creative acts. Information will be presented to document clear understanding of each creative act while appreciating the supernatural accomplishments and greatness of the Creator and His creation. Remarkably, each creative act was timed flawlessly to prepare for the needs of subsequent creations.

The book of Genesis, authored by Moses, is the foundation of the Bible and provides definitive details regarding the beginning of the universe. One only needs to read the first verse of the first chapter of Genesis to identify the Divine Creator, "In the beginning, God created the heavens and the Earth." Genesis reveals the creator to man and, additionally, shows our sinful condition and our need for a redemptive plan.

To accept creation it is necessary to recognize the Creator (*Elohim*, the Hebrew word for God in Genesis 1:1). Without accepting that God existed eternally, the reality of creation or belief in his inspired Word will likely be doubted. Nowhere in the Bible is the pre-creation existence of God questioned. Everything else in the world had a beginning but God has always been. "Before the mountains were brought forth, or ever you had formed the Earth and the world, from everlasting to everlasting you are God" (Psalm 90:2). If one believes Genesis 1:1, belief in the remainder of the Bible should not be troublesome. If, indeed, God created all things, should He not also be able to control everything and keep His creation in balance? Nonetheless, there have always been, and will continue to be, many who refuse to embrace the clear tenants of God's Word and attempt to explain creation through evolutionary or other concepts. This book will not endeavor to influence this group from their faulty positions but will pursue the biblical authenticity of divine creation. There are no valid disagreements between the Bible and true science. Contradictions between God's works and God's Word do not exist.

Elohim denotes the divine fullness and omnipotence of a Triune God. The Trinity was wholly involved in creation. God the Father was the Architect, God the Son the Instrument and God the Holy Spirit the Energizer. Light was created when God spoke, clearly the act of an architect. "And God said, Let there be light, and there was light" (Genesis 1:3). Seven additional verses in Genesis 1 reveal that God spoke creation into existence with the words, "God said." Hebrews 11:3 states, "By faith we understand that the universe was created by the word of God, so that what is seen was not made out of things that are visible." Thus, it is apparent that the universe was spoken into existence by God.

The New Testament further supports creation by the Trinity. In John 1:1-3, the Word is presented as synonymous with God. "In the beginning was the word, and the Word was with God, and the Word was God. He was in the beginning with God. All things were made through him and without him was not any thing made that was made." Verse 14 states, "And the Word became flesh and dwelt among us, we have seen His glory, glory as of the only Son from the Father, full of grace and truth." The Word became flesh so Christ was involved. In Colossians 1:16, the Apostle Paul expanded on Christ's creative input. "For by Him [Christ] all things were created, in heaven and on earth, visible and invisible, whether thrones or dominions or rulers or authorities—all things were created through him and for him." The involvement of the Holy Spirit is seen in Genesis 1:2, "The Earth was without form and void, and darkness was over the face of the deep. And the Spirit of God was hovering over the face of the waters." Although the various creative acts by the three members of the Trinity are not all identified individually, it is evident from scripture that all three persons of the Godhead were involved.

The actual date or time of creation is not given in the Bible. We do know that God made all things without the use of preexisting materials (*creatio ex nihilo*). A question that has been of interest to scholars is, "Why did God create?" Only God knows the answer to this question; however, the following reasons have been postulated:

1. He may have created for His pleasure. The previously stated verse (Colossians 1:16) denotes that man was created for the Lord, He may receive joy from man's obedience, worship, activities, and pursuits.

2. God may have created to reveal Himself and His Glory. This view has some credence since creation was the first revelation of God to the world. "By the word of the Lord the heavens were made, and by the breath of his mouth all their host. For he spoke, and it came to be; he commanded, and it stood firm" (Psalm 33, 6, 9).

3. Creation allowed the revelation of the person of God. Without the creation of man, there would have been no need for Christ the Savior, who appeared as the image of God. "He is the image of the invisible God, the firstborn of all creation" (Colossians 1:15).

Likely, the greatest ambivalence concerning the entire Genesis creation account is the length of days during which the various creative events occurred. There have been valiant efforts to diminish God's supernatural creative powers by presenting differing theories, advocating that each day was a long, indefinite period of time. The Bible is abundantly clear that creation was completed in six literal 24-hour days. The Hebrew word, *yôm,* is translated as *day* throughout Genesis 1. Further, the word *yôm* is translated as a 24-hour day several hundred times in the Old Testament. When *yôm* is associated with a number in the Old Testament it always designates a 24-hour period. For each creative day the phrase "the evening and morning," again, clearly indicates 24-hour day periods. Twenty-four-hour days are also evident in Exodus 20:8-11, "Remember the Sabbath day, to keep it holy. Six days you shall labor, and do all your work, but the seventh day is a Sabbath to the Lord your God. On it you shall not do any work, you, or your son, or your daughter, your male servant, or your female servant, or your livestock, or the sojourner who is within your gates. For in six days the Lord made heaven and earth, the sea, and all that is in them, and rested the seventh day. Therefore the Lord blessed the Sabbath day and made it holy."

After six days, God's perfect creative efforts were completed. He is now no longer creating but preserving His creation. "And he is before all things, and in him all things hold together" (Colossians 1:17). Sadly, evolutionists, as well as those advancing other non-scriptural theories, make great efforts to increase the time periods in creation days. Longer periods of time would accommodate their false claims for evolutionary developments to occur. Regardless of these unscientific attempts, there is no biblical evidence to support that creation took place over extended periods of time. But, there is overwhelming support for the biblical creation account portraying six 24-hour days.

God has not provided every detail of his creation. However, adequate scriptural documentation is available to conclude, *God created*! Science attempts to explain origins through the chance of evolution and time gaps. The Bible reveals the beginnings of all things through creation by an omnipotent God. Genesis 1 states repeatedly after specific days of creation, "God saw that it was good." Yes, God's marvelous creation was good and continues to provide joy for mankind. The real question concerning what one accepts in the explanation of origins is, How big is your God?

"The Lord by wisdom founded the Earth; by understanding he established the heavens; by his knowledge the deeps broke open, and the clouds drop down the dew" (Proverbs 3:19-20)

Chapter 1

Day One—The Heavens and the Earth,
Light Separated from Darkness

"In the beginning, God created the heavens and the Earth. The Earth was without form and void, and darkness was over the face of the deep. And the Spirit of God was hovering over the face of the waters. And God said, Let there be light, and there was light. And God saw that the light was good. And God separated the light from the darkness. God called the light Day, and the darkness he called Night. And there was evening and there was morning, the first day" (Genesis 1:1-5).

The Earth was initially a chaotic, unorganized mass of matter. It consisted of an immense sodden mixture of water, mud, and rocks. Darkness prevailed, temperatures were not controlled, and no life was in sight anywhere. If anyone would have been present to observe this huge hapless accumulation of material, a quick exit from this confusing scene would have been highly probable.

What could possibly be done under these seemingly hopeless conditions? Who could ever bring order to this monumental unsightly mess? Ah, stop worrying! In this seemingly impossible panorama appears the Creator, the Almighty God. Indeed, everything was, and continues to be, under control.

One is quickly set at ease with the summary statement in Genesis 1:1 which introduces the forthcoming six days of creation. On the first day, God created time (in the beginning), space (the heavens), and matter (the Earth). His initial creative act involved formation of the heavens and earth from nonexistent material. Although there are those who wish to place a large time interval between Genesis 1:1 and subsequent verses, this belief (gap theory) has no credence. Proponents of this theory maintain that an earlier earth, which they believe is mentioned in verse 1, was totally ravaged due to divine judgement for Lucifer's sins (also known as Lucifer's Flood). Thereafter, the Earth was allegedly re-created in six days. This view presents some difficult problems. If God created the heavens and earth from nothing, there would not have been previous material to re-create, as proposed by the gap theorists. Fossils found in sedimentary rocks by gap theory advocates, purported to be from the previous earth, are similar to those found in our current earth. Thus, if these plants and animals existed on the earlier earth, they had to be created again during the later 6-day creation. This would indicate that plants and animals that developed during a long previous period on the first earth, as needed for belief in the gap theory, were destroyed suddenly in a devastating flood only to be replaced with similar species over a very short period of time, as occurred in creation. The gap theory is an unacceptable attempt at integrating evolutionary biology with geology. This theory provides no support to evolutionists nor is it accepted by today's knowledgeable geologists. Although still advocated by a few biblical scholars, the gap theory presents serious fallacies and is no longer considered credible by most informed scientists and Christians.

THE EARTH

The huge mass of earthen material, created without form and void as described in Genesis 1:1, needed to be fashioned and refined. At that time, emptiness of darkness prevailed and God created order from disorder. The Spirit hovered over the waters that covered the Earth preparing them for the second day of creation. The dry land, oceans, and mountains would not appear until the third day. It would surely have been possible for God to create everything, including all living creatures, on the first day. Could it be that he waited until the last of the six creation days to create man to establish six work days and one day for rest?

To appreciate fully the amplitude of God's creative work in completing the Earth, it would be advantageous to understand some scientific facts regarding this planet. Current knowledge about the Earth has increased due to space exploration flights. The Earth is the fifth largest planet in the solar system and is located third in distance from the sun. It is 7,926 miles in diameter and the only planet known to support life. Although most of the Earth's makeup is inaccessible, its content has been conjectured through seismic waves and examinations of volcanic lava. The central core is thought to consist of iron or nickel/ iron. Temperature at the core is estimated to be 13,500° F, hotter than the sun's surface. The next layer is believed to be composed of silicon, magnesium, iron, calcium, aluminum, and oxygen. Above this is an upper layer consisting of olivine (silicate of magnesium and iron), pyroxene (iron and magnesium silicate), calcium, and magnesium. The surface (crust) of the Earth is mostly quartz (silicon dioxide), and feldspar (combination of several hard crystalline minerals). Earthquakes occur when there is a sudden release of deeply stored energy that produces movement of the Earth's rocky surface plates.

Minimal variations in temperature allow for sustenance of life. The temperatures on the Earth vary only slightly from day to night. In addition to warming of the Earth by the sun, heat retention by ocean waters also aids in keeping temperatures stable. The Earth is surrounded by a gravitational field. This field produces a downward force (gravity) on objects near or on the Earth.

There are weak magnetic fields in the outer core of the Earth caused by electric currents. These field lines radiate between the north and south magnetic poles of the Earth trapping charged particles, thus forming the magnetosphere. The magnetosphere extends thousands of miles in space. Some scientists believe these magnetic field lines are weakening and may disappear between the years of 3,000 and 4,000.

God created the Earth, one of the smaller planets, before He made the other planets, sun, moon, and stars. Why did God create the Earth prior to speaking the other planets into existence later, on day four? Perhaps God wished to identify the Earth as the most important planet. Here is where He would place man, the one to be created in His image. His ultimate creation, man, would be given dominion over the Earth and would worship the Creator. The Earth is the planet to which He would send His Son to pay the price for man's sins on Calvary. This is the same planet where God the Son will return at the rapture to claim his redeemed children.

The foregoing superficial review of the Earth fails to describe amply the marvels of this magnificent planet. Hopefully, sufficient information has been provided to recognize and appreciate the greatness of this phenomenal initial creative act.

THE HEAVENS

The heavens were differentiated into three parts on the first day of creation. The Third Heaven is a wonderful creation of which we have only limited knowledge. The Apostle Paul described this incredible site as follows: "I must go on boasting. Though there is nothing to be gained by it, I will go on to visions and revelations of the Lord. I know a man in Christ who fourteen years ago was caught up to the third heaven—whether in the body or out of the body I do not know, God knows. And I know that this man was caught up into paradise— whether in the body or out of the body I do not know, God knows—and he heard things that cannot be told, which man may not utter" (2 Corinthians 12:1-4). One thing we do know about the Third Heaven is that, in the beginning, God had populated it with numerous angels called the Sons of God. "Where were you when I laid the foundation of the Earth? Tell me, if you have understanding. Who determined its measurements—surely you know! Or who stretched the line upon it? On what were its bases sunk, or who laid its cornerstone, when the morning stars sang together and all the sons of God shouted for joy?" (Job 38:4-7).

The Second Heaven may be thought of as outer space, where the heavenly bodies would appear on the fourth day of creation. The atmospheric area surrounding the Earth where clouds appear, as well as the place where birds fly, is the First Heaven. These atmospheric layers will be described further in the next chapter.

LIGHT

During the first day of creation, God also produced light. This was His second act after creating the Earth earlier in the day. God separated the light from darkness and He called the light day and the darkness night, pronouncing that He had fashioned evening and morning of the first day. This indicates that the twenty-four hour revolution of the Earth had begun as it continues to this day.

The light God created on the first day did not come from the sun which would appear on the fourth day. Therefore, the light in Genesis 1:3 was likely a unique cosmic illumination that provided energy to augment the next days of creation. God, Himself, is identified as being light in 1 John 1:5, "This is the message we have heard from him and proclaim to you, that God is light, and in him is no darkness at all." This first light would make God's creation visible and life possible. It is encouraging to know that God's initial act of producing life-creating and life-sustaining light, the light of the world, would provide the needs of His ultimate creation, man.

The creative acts of the first day set the stage for the next step in God's plan. He had separated the light from darkness establishing regulated days. Further, God's cosmic light provided the capability to view each created component as well as produced energy needed for future activities.

The now refined earth had abundant soil infused with appropriate ingredients for future plant growth. Various minerals, gems, and chemicals were placed within the Earth to provide for man's future needs. Gravitational forces were generated to hold everything in place and magnetic fields were prepared to allow future cosmic activities and even provide navigational sensors for migrating birds.

The magnificent Third Heaven, which will not be revealed fully until those who have been born again go to their eternal home, was created and is awaiting God's children. Christians should be encouraged that God, on the first day of creation, had already prepared a place for His children. The First Heaven (earth's atmosphere), immediately surrounding the Earth is now ready for completion during the second day, God's next creative act.

Formation of the heavens and earth plus production of God's cosmic light all occurred on the first day of creation. This was a monumental day for creative acts; God saw that it was good and, thus, concluded the first day of creation. The Earth was now created and energized, and prepared for additional creative acts in preparation for man's supremacy over the Earth.

> *"Praise the LORD. Praise God in his sanctuary; praise him in his mighty heavens"* (Psalm 150:1).

Chapter 2

Day Two—The Firmament or Atmosphere

"And God said, Let there be an expanse in the midst of the waters, and let it separate the waters from the waters. And God made the expanse and separated the waters that were under the expanse from the waters that were above the expanse. And it was so. And God called the expanse Heaven. And there was evening and there was morning, the second day" (Gen. 1:6-8).

Although the Earth had taken on form and order, water remained on its surface and in the surrounding planetary space. The full potential of the Earth would be impossible with water literally everywhere. Also, the space above the Earth needed to be organized to meet the future requirements of plants, animals, and man. Thus, on the second day of creation, God separated the waters.

God divided the waters into two locations, one above and the other on the Earth. The expanse above the Earth is called the firmament in some Bible translations, or is also known as the First Heaven (described in the previous chapter). The Bible does not indicate what form of water was present in the firmament but it is thought to have been a heavy vapor that surrounded the Earth. This vapor would serve as a filter for harmful light rays from the sun (to appear on day four), would encourage plant growth (plants to appear on day three), and contribute to ensuring uniform climatic conditions. Since there was no rain prior to the universal Noahic flood, the vapor likely differed from that now found in the atmosphere. There is no mention of clouds in the Bible until later in Genesis when God told Noah, "I have set my bow in the cloud, and it shall be a sign of the covenant between me and the Earth" (Genesis 9:13).

In biblical revelations the term firmament means the heavens or something stretched out. Currently, the firmament or First Heaven is generally called the atmosphere. The atmosphere is divided into four major layers differentiated by temperature changes, chemical makeup, wind activity, and density. The four levels consist of a blanket of air stretching approximately four hundred miles above the surface of the Earth. Descriptions of these layers follow, starting with the layer nearest the surface of the Earth:

TROPOSPHERE

This layer extends four to eleven miles above the Earth and is the densest portion of the atmosphere. Weather formation occurs in this region, and rising and falling air pressures are common. Essentially, all water vapor and solid particles arising from the Earth's surface are found here. All animals and plants live either in the troposphere, on the Earth, within the Earth, or in bodies of water on the Earth. Temperatures in this atmospheric layer decrease with height and measure -76° F near the top. A thin layer, the tropopause, separates the troposphere from the next higher layer, the stratosphere.

STRATOSPHERE

The stratosphere is twenty miles deep and is a dry, less dense area than the troposphere. Jet aircraft frequently fly in the stratosphere because it is highly stable. Air movement in this area is mostly horizontal producing flowing rivers or jet streams. These jet streams can change weather patterns in the troposphere below. Temperatures at the top of the stratosphere are regulated by absorption of ultraviolet radiation and increase to readings similar to those at sea level. This rise in temperature is due to the ozone layer located in this area, a reactive form of oxygen that absorbs ultraviolet rays from the sun. Volcanic debris may enter and remain in the stratosphere for several years and, then, eventually settles to earth again. Ninety-nine percent of air is located in the two major lower layers of the atmosphere, the troposphere and stratosphere. Another thin layer, the stratopause, separates the stratosphere from the next higher level, the mesosphere.

MESOSPHERE

The mesosphere is 25 miles deep and temperatures in this layer are as low as -173° F and air currents are mixed. Chemicals in this area are active as they absorb energy from the sun. This is the level of the atmosphere where meteor or rock fragments burn up during entry from space, with subsequent falling of the debris to the surface of the Earth. A thin layer, the mesopause, separates the mesosphere from the next higher level of the atmosphere, the thermosphere. Together, the stratosphere, stratopause, mesosphere, and mesopause are called the lower atmosphere. The lower atmosphere prevents most harmful ultraviolet rays and radiation from reaching the surface of the Earth.

THERMOSPHERE

The thermosphere is the largest layer of the atmosphere, being 161 miles in depth. Temperatures in this area fluctuate greatly. Here reduced numbers of molecules retain heat from the sun and, additionally, considerable energy from the solar system is absorbed and radiates heat. Thus, temperatures of 440° F to as high as 1,832° F have been postulated. The higher temperatures at the upper levels are in the area that is nearer to the sun. Chemical reactions occur more rapidly here due to increased heat. This is the layer of the atmosphere where auroras occur. Auroras (borealis or australis), which are luminous displays, result when solar wind causes high-energy atomic particles from the sun to collide with gas molecules. These are also known as northern or southern lights and they appear as colored, flickering, glowing exhibitions in the sky. The thermosphere, also called the upper atmosphere, absorbs highly energetic photons from the sun and reflects radio waves enhancing long-distance communications.

The atmosphere is composed primarily of nitrogen (79%), oxygen (20%), and argon (less than 1%), necessary for maintenance of life on earth. Other important components, although in smaller amounts, are water, ozone (greenhouse gasses), and carbon dioxide. Water vapor is added to the atmosphere through evaporation from oceans, lakes, rivers, ponds, streams, soil, and plants. These sources of water determine humidity levels on the Earth.

Information about the area above the thermosphere is limited. This layer is called the exosphere which continues upward into space beyond 400 miles and has been estimated to stretch to a height of from 3,500 to 40,000 miles. This area contains interplanetary gases, consisting primarily of low levels of hydrogen and helium.

What is the value of the atmosphere for plants, animals, and man? God designed the Earth with large reservoirs of water and an extensive overhead blanket of a mixture of oxygen and nitrogen gasses, all necessary to sustain life. The atmosphere, solar energy, and magnetic fields all help support life on earth. Functions served by the atmosphere include absorption of excess energy from the sun, recycling of water and chemicals, and interactions with magnetic fields to control climate. The area for origination of weather patterns was now completed and temperature regulation was possible.

An area for shielding the Earth from damaging debris from space was established. The atmosphere was designed carefully to protect against high-energy radiation, harmful ultraviolet rays, and exposure to the frigid vacuum found in space. Interesting lighting displays for man's enjoyment were developed and areas for long-distant communications were ready for man's eventual needs. Vast open spaces were prepared and provided with adequate resources to ensure survival of flying creatures. After creating the firmament, a unique and remarkable atmosphere was available to sustain the physical well-being of plants, animals, and man and, thus, day two of creation was completed. Next in God's perfect creative sequence, He will separate dry land from the seas and produce vegetation.

> "*The heavens declare the glory of God, and the sky above proclaims his handiwork*" (Psalm 19:1).

Chapter 3

Day Three—Dry Land, Seas, and Vegetation

"And God said, Let the waters under the heavens be gathered together into one place, and let the dry land appear. And it was so. God called the dry land Earth, and the waters that were gathered together he called Seas. And God saw that it was good. And God said, Let the Earth sprout vegetation, plants yielding seed, and fruit trees bearing fruit in which is their seed, each according to its kind, on the Earth. And it was so. The Earth brought forth vegetation, plants yielding seed according to their own kinds, and trees bearing fruit in which is their seed, each according to its kind. And God saw that it was good. And there was evening and there was morning, the third day" (Genesis 1:9-13).

Obviously, no people were there but excitement was in the air. What would be the next logical creative acts? God had completed planet earth with a life-sustaining mixture of water and soil, atmospheric growth elements, light for energy, climate control, and protection from harmful radiation and ultraviolet rays, plus safety from falling debris from space.

What should God do next? It appears that production of food and beauty for future inhabitants, both animals and man, would be appropriate. God is never confused and he certainly was not perplexed regarding the next creative acts necessary for His perfect plan. An inhabitable universe, plants, animals, man, and a Heavenly Home. Could anyone improve on that?

Thus, on the third day of creation, God made an additional division, separating water from dry land. He called the water seas and the dry land earth. The extent of the original waters and dry land is unknown since there was some rearrangement of boundaries following the cataclysmic Noahic flood. Some Bible scholars believe that, following this pivotal event, there are now larger bodies of water than created originally. The information in this chapter describes the Earth's current bodies of water.

OCEANS AND SEAS

Oceanographers generally consider that there is a single world ocean separated by several continental masses. They divide the parts of this large worldwide body of water into the Atlantic, Pacific, Indian, and Arctic Oceans. These are subdivided further into smaller bodies of water known as seas, gulfs, or bays. Current oceans cover approximately 71% of the Earth's surface. Elements in the oceans comprise over 96% oxygen and hydrogen with minimal amounts of dissolved chlorine, sodium, and other salts. About 97% of ocean waters consist of saltwater, most having a temperature just above freezing at 39° F.

The deepest spot in the ocean is called the Challenger Deep located in the Mariana Trench of the Pacific Ocean. This area reaches a depth of 35,802 feet producing pressure of more than eight tons per square inch. The longest mountain range is the Mid-Ocean Ridge found in the middle of the Atlantic Ocean extending into the Pacific Ocean. The Mid-Ocean Ridge is four times longer than a combination of the Andes, Rockies, and Himalayas mountains. Ninety percent of all volcanic activity occurs in the oceans and an inactive volcano, which is also the tallest mountain in the world (33,465 feet), is located partly underwater in Mauna Kea, Hawaii. The largest waterfall is in the ocean located in the Denmark Strait. Earthquakes, known as tsunamis, occur infrequently in ocean waters.

Essentially all continents are surrounded by submerged, sloping plains termed continental shelves. Plentiful stores of valuable petroleum, commercial sand, gravel deposits, and fishery resources are found throughout these shelf areas. An intricate relationship exists between the oceans and the atmosphere above. When winds incite waves, water droplets evaporate into the air removing heat from the oceans. Storage of these water molecules in the atmosphere helps regulate climatic conditions, including production of rain.

The oceans and other bodies of water provide recreational areas, transport avenues, seafood, jewels, and building materials (sand, shells and coral). Various useful minerals, including salt, bromine, and magnesium, are also harvested from the world's bodies of water. Further, the oceans contain large quantities of deuterium (hydrogen isotope) which could be converted into energy through future development of nuclear fusion reactors.

TIDES

Tides are periodic rising or falling ocean surfaces energized by changes in gravitational forces from the sun and moon. There are generally two high and two low tide waves daily. Since there are changes in distances to the moon and stars, due to elliptical orbits of the Earth, tidal wave forces vary. The highest known tide reaches over 43 feet and is located in the Bay of Fundy east of New Brunswick, Canada; however, the Baltic, Mediterranean, and Caribbean Seas are nearly tideless. Tides produce several helpful benefits including distribution of marine animals and plants, as well as regulating animal feeding and reproduction (spawning) activities,

On the third day of creation, God also separated the soil from water and made all plants including grasses, shrubs, food producing crops, and trees. It is thought that these plants were created fully matured bearing flowers, vegetables, fruits, and seeds. Further, most scholars agree that vegetation was present over the entire earth, not only in the Garden of Eden.

SOIL

Soil is the top layer of the Earth's surface and consists of disintegrated rocks. Depending upon specific content, soil types may be clay, silt, sand, gravel, stone, or various combinations of these elements. How soil particles are arranged determines its density and numbers of pore spaces which allow water and air retention required for plant growth. Humus is the moist nutrient-laden layer of organic matter often found on the surface of soil, made up of decaying plant and animal materials. In addition to organic matter, productive growing soil contains silicon, aluminum, iron, oxygen, calcium, magnesium, sodium, and potassium. Use of chemical fertilizers and organic matter, such as animal manure or decomposed vegetation, increases soil fertility. For specific plants, soil acidity may be increased by adding sulfuric acid or decreased by using calcium carbonate.

PLANTS

Plants differ from animals in that they contain chlorophyll, usually remain in one location, have no sensory systems for responding to external stimuli, and have firm cellulose-containing protective coverings. Plant cell structures and reproductive methods also vary from those of animals. Chlorophyl is a green pigment present in chloroplast-laden plant cells, which is essential for the photosynthetic process to occur. Photosynthesis results when a series of reactions within a plant cause light energy to be converted into chemical or food components. Growth in plants continues throughout their lives.

Many plants have an intrinsic timing mechanism which allows them to coordinate various growth activities with the different seasons. Some depend upon a period of exposure to cold temperatures, called vernalization, to bloom or stimulate seed germination. A few of these include tulips and winter wheat. Vernalization ensures that plants do not produce until the winter season has ended.

Plant leaves come in numerous shapes and types. In dry deserts, the leaves of some plants roll up to form a spine as seen in cacti. In this environment, ordinary leaves have been sacrificed in favor of water conservation. These plants have heavy exterior protective coverings to protect them from damage and curtail excessive water evaporation. In desert plants, much of the photosynthesis process is carried out by the chlorophyll-containing cells in the stems. If they have leaves, they are generally very small or orient their edges toward the sun during hot temperatures to reduce evaporation of fluids. In contrast, the leaves of tropical rain forest shrubs are large and broad, especially at the bottom of the forest canopy where light is scarce and water plentiful.

FOOD PLANTS

Vegetables and crops provide food for animals and man and are produced from plant leaves, roots, bulbs, tubers, buds, flowers, seeds, and stems. These plants are important for ensuring adequate diets that supply excellent sources of vitamins, minerals, and chemicals. Vegetables consist primarily of water which makes them low in caloric content. Crop plants or animal foods may consist of seeds such as corn, oats, wheat, and soybeans, or they may be used as green or dry foods including corn, grasses, or legumes such as alfalfa. Food plants are usually annuals and need to be replanted every year. Different food plants require varying soil and climatic conditions, thus suiting them for dissimilar areas around the world.

FLOWERS

There are about 200,000 kinds of flowers in the world. Flowers are actually the reproductive organs of angiosperms (flowering plants). Producing seeds through sexual reproduction is the primary function of flowers. Additional attributes are to provide beauty and food. Although plants grow continuously, flowers do not; they have maturity limits. The majority of flowers are bisexual, having both pistils (male parts) and stamens (female parts). However, some are unisexual having either stamens or pistils. Some bisexual flowers are self-fertilizing while others are not, since their sexual parts may not mature at the same time or the plant's pollen cannot fertilize its own ovules. Whether bisexual or unisexual, pollination must take place and occurs through wind currents, animal and human transport, or by visiting nectar-collecting insects.

Following are some interesting created intrinsic marvels of several flowers. The largest flower in the world (*raflesia arnoldi*) grows in Indonesia and weighs 15 pounds while the smallest, the duckweed, is found floating in streams throughout the world and can be seen only with a microscope. The two primary indicators for stimulating flowering are photoperiod (light intensity and day-length) and temperature. Poinsettias are forced to bloom early for the Christmas holidays by using required temperature and day-length. Floral clocks are known to function in some daisies; they open and close at certain times each morning and evening. Many plants open their leaves during the day and close them at night. They need the energy of sunlight to drive photosynthetic reactions that convert carbon dioxide and water into sugars, and release oxygen. Bulb growers in Holland, who want to produce year-round tulips, drive around at night on tractors equipped with huge booms of red lights to illuminate the plants and fool them into flowering.

TREES

It has been estimated that there are over 40,000 species of trees in the world. Trees produce flowers, fruits, nuts, coconuts, pods, or syrup. Reproduction occurs by seeds, cuttings, cones, and nuts. Trees discharge large amounts of oxygen into the atmosphere. A single large tree can lift and discharge 100 gallons of water into the atmosphere daily. Trees grow in all sizes, coastal redwoods reaching over 360 feet tall and giant sequoias weighing over 2,000 tons.

Most trees produce flowers but they are often not seen nor recognized. Seed formation is similar to that of flowering plants with the exception that some trees reproduce through production of fruits or cones. Tree seeds are spread by several methods including fruit dropping to the ground or squirrels burying nuts. Many trees produce seeds that have special attachment adaptations allowing them to be transported long distances by wind, water, animals, or people.

Trees have the innate ability to survive under adverse conditions. When under stress they will shed leaves, flowers, fruits, or even entire branches. Newly planted unstaked trees generally grow stronger due to exposure to repeated strain from winds. Roots of most trees do not grow deep but remain in the top 12 inches of soil; however, they may extend to three times beyond the width of their branches. In addition to providing food, trees have numerous other commercial uses. Wood has been used throughout history for building and heating. Tree bark and fruit provide several medicinal products, many still under investigation. Trees provide sound and snow barriers as well as protective nesting sites for hundreds of birds and other animals.

SEEDS

A seed is the embryo of a plant that can produce another similar plant. There are approximately 250,000 known seeds in the world. Sizes of seeds have no direct relationship to the sizes of plants. The double coconut tree produces a seed that weighs up to 50 pounds while 800,000 orchid seeds weigh only one ounce. As discussed previously, seeds may be distributed by fruit, nuts, animals, people, wind, water, transport vehicles, and ships. Further, some seeds are equipped with special dispersion features that allow long distance wind, water, animal, and human distribution.

For seeds to grow they must undergo a process called germination. Favorable conditions for germination require fertile soil, adequate water, ample oxygen, and proper temperatures. Some seeds require long daylight periods while others need shorter days, thus allocating germination times to specific seasonal periods. A few plants produce seeds that have very hard protective coverings. To ensure germination, these coverings must be penetrated. Such seeds may be carried along waterways where they are exposed to sharp rocks or sand which damages their hard surfaces making them porous. Thereafter, the seeds will germinate if exposed to a fertile growth medium and moisture.

Day three was, indeed, a significant day of creation. The dry land was separated from the waters, fertile soil was provided, and thousands of plants were created. Oceans, now in place, contained valuable minerals, building supplies, and petroleum reserves. Droplets of ocean water absorbed into the atmosphere facilitated climate control. Tides were established to assist in movement of plants and allow reproduction in fishes. Vast bodies of water were designed to provide a future home for an abundance of sea creatures.

The separated soil was supplied with proper nutrients to ensure plant growth. Numerous kinds of plants were fashioned for enjoyment and for ultimate sources of food and energy for animals and man. Diverse maturation times for different plants were designed to provide specific needs at various times. Besides producing foods, plants were available to provide fibers, drugs, oils, latex, pigments, resins, coal, clothing, fuels, and raw materials for various products. Plant seeds were a ready source for animal and human foods, cooking oils, beverages (coffee, cocoa), detergents, paints, varnishes, and decorative crafts. Vast nesting sites for birds and other animals had been perfected. A unique method was devised to ensure the production of oxygen and removal of carbon dioxide by plants.

Thus ended the third day of creation. Now planet earth is prepared for provision of an enormous energy source to promote growth and expedite food-generating photosensitization in plants. Defined day and night periods and specific seasons will be required to sustain life for the multiplicity of created plants. Insects and other animals should be available to facilitate plant reproduction through pollination. Magnetic forces will be needed to actuate high and low ocean tides.

Having the Earth prepared for day four of creation, it will be exciting to note what takes place next. What additional creative acts will be provided to continue preparation of the Earth for man's eventual habitation? How encouraging to realize that our all-knowing God understood fully what was needed and He would do exactly what was required for continuing His perfect creation plan.

> *"The Earth is the LORD'S and the fullness thereof, the*
> *world and those who dwell therein"* (Psalm 24:1).

Chapter 4

Day Four—Sun, Moon, Stars, Seasons, Days, and Years

"And God said, Let there be lights in the expanse of the heavens to separate the day from the night. And let them be for signs and for seasons, and for days and years, and let them be lights in the expanse of the heavens to give light upon the Earth. And it was so. And God made the two great lights—the greater light to rule the day and the lesser light to rule the night—and the stars. And God set them in the expanse of the heavens to give light on the Earth, to rule over the day and over the night, and to separate the light from the darkness. And God saw that it was good. And there was evening and there was morning, the fourth day" (Genesis 1:14-19).

Immense numbers of plants were growing on the Earth following the previous day's creation. On this fourth day, God determined that an energy source for sustenance of all this vegetation was necessary. He also saw a need to establish seasons, days, and years to institute orderly growth periods and time patterns; so on the fourth day of creation, God spoke the sun, moon, and stars into existence. The previous cosmic light source that God created on the first day would now be replaced with the sun and stars.

SUN

Several new facts about the solar system have been learned in recent years from studies conducted during various space exploration flights. The sun is one of over 100 billion stars located in the Milky Way, the portion of the galaxy that can be observed from earth. It is considered the center of the universe and produces light energy for maintenance of physical and biological life on earth. Being the largest object in the solar system, the sun has a radius measuring 432,000 miles, approximately 109 times the size of the Earth. Scientists describe its content as plasma, neither solid nor totally gaseous, consisting of approximately 70% hydrogen and 28% helium, plus minimal other materials. Located about 92,960 million miles from the Earth, light from the sun travels at 186,282 miles per second and takes eight minutes to reach our planet.

The sun rotates on its axis about once a month and it vibrates continually, producing complex sound waves while releasing energy for the solar system. Energy from the sun is produced in its core and is generated through nuclear fusion which occurs when two atomic nuclei join to form a new larger nucleus. Temperature in the core is more than 28 million degrees F while the surface or photosphere is about $10,400°$ F. It has been estimated that continual energy output from the sun is 386 billion megawatts.

Often, the wonder of sunlight is taken for granted without examining its numerous beneficial facets. Thus, some of the major attributes of light will be reviewed. The study of light is known as optics. Since the 1600s many discoveries have been made about light. Light is radiant energy that travels freely through space at a speed dependent upon several factors. The normal rate of speed for unimpeded light rays has been determined to be 186,282 miles per second; however, any substances (primarily atoms) in the path of light will impede its traveling speed. Types of light include the visible spectra, infrared rays, radio waves, ultraviolet rays, and x-rays. Light is usually described as occurring in waves which consist of a combination of electric and magnetic fields and are, thus, referred to as electromagnetic waves. In addition to waves, light also appears as small particles called photons. The energy carried by waves and photons determines the color emitted by light. The various types of light are differentiated according to the length of the electromagnetic waves. The small part of radiant energy that can be seen is visible light. Electromagnetic waves vary in length for the different colors of light observed. The shortest visible waves are violet (380-425 nanometers) while the longest are red (700-750 nanometers). Between these are all the other colors of the visible light spectrum. Ultraviolet rays have wave lengths just below the visible light spectrum while those shorter than these are known as x-rays. Infrared rays are slightly longer than the visible red waves and microwaves, and radio waves are at the long end of the electromagnetic spectrum.

The different colors present in light are determined by the atoms contained in the electromagnetic waves and can be differentiated by passing them through an instrument called a spectrometer. Colors may also be separated by passing the rays through a simple prism. There are luminescent materials that glow in the dark following exposure to light energy. Some of these materials glow in the dark for considerable periods of time after receiving light energy.

Light may be absorbed by some surfaces, thereby producing chemical effects. Strong light can cause these materials to fade or change color. Further, food production in plants, called photosynthesis, is the result of chemical actions that occur following light stimulation.

Most people take light for granted and assume it has always been and will always be. But the intricacies of light are extremely fascinating and much is still to be learned about its actions, functions, and benefits. Without an overview of the tremendous attributes of light, it would be difficult to appreciate fully the magnitude of this major creative act. The creation of light on the first day has, indeed, been highly significant and will continue to be so in the ages ahead.

In addition to the production of light, there are continuing weather conditions that take place on the sun's surface. Sunspots are the coolest areas on the sun where huge and powerful hurricanes occur, having lifting winds of 3,000 miles per hour. Massive tornadoes occur on the sun that are 1,200 times more powerful that those recorded on earth.

The sun's solar winds consist of charged particles that fly into the solar system from the sun's surface at high speeds of up to 900,000 miles per hour. Solar flares release even more energy and can cause power line surges and radio interference on earth as well as be dangerous to space craft. The sun has a strong magnetic field that extends far into the solar system, which has been described by astronomers as very complicated and not fully understood.

MOON

The moon is the brightest solar body seen at night and the only natural satellite of the Earth. Although the moon generates no light of its own, it reflects sunlight. It is considerably smaller than the Earth with a radius of 1,080 miles, 27% the size of the Earth. A weak gravitational force from the moon causes tidal waves on the Earth. The moon is located approximately 238,890 miles from the Earth; a distance that is increasing 1.5 inches each year. The light-colored areas seen on the surface of the moon are rugged highlands and the dark spots are craters, formed primarily from collisions with meteoroids, asteroids, or comets. Temperatures on the moon vary greatly, from -280° F at night to 260° F during daytime, while they remain constantly at -400° F in deep craters and at the moon's poles.

There is no life on the moon and the sky above always appears black. The moon rotates consistently on its axis once every 29.5 days, and orbits around the Earth about every 27.3 days. Like the Earth, the moon consists of three layers. The surface crust is 43 miles thick, composed mostly of rocks. Dense rocks, that are rich in iron and magnesium, make up the large middle layer. The inner core of the moon contains primarily iron and sulphur.

Eclipses result when the Earth, sun, and moon are located in a straight line. A lunar (moon) eclipse is observed when the Earth moves between the sun and the moon causing the shadow of the Earth to appear on the moon, occurring only during the time of a full moon. When the moon moves between the sun and earth, the moon's shadow is seen on the Earth producing a solar eclipse, which occurs only during a new moon period.

STARS

Stars are hot, light-emitting spheres of gas that are bound together by gravitational forces. Their light is generated by nuclear energy and brightness varies greatly among stars. They differ in sizes from one-tenth to over 50 times the volume of the sun. Most stars are gaseous and composed of over 90% hydrogen. This hydrogen is changed to helium through nuclear fusion causing visible light. This reaction is similar to that generated by a hydrogen bomb, producing amounts of light according to the size of each star. Stars twinkle since their light is disrupted while traveling through the turbulent atmosphere of the Earth.

Stars visible from earth are in the area known as the Milky Way while myriads of others beyond this vast expanse have never been seen. Astronomers have estimated that there may be at least 80 to 100 billion other galaxies in the extended universe, each containing billions of stars.

In addition to the sun, moon, and stars, the planets and other heavenly bodies were most likely created on the fourth day also. Besides the Earth, there are seven other known planets plus untold asteroids, comets, and meteors. Each planet's makeup and movements are as complicated and fascinating as those of the Earth; they have their individual weather and seasons. The inner planets, located nearer to the sun, consist of Mercury, Venus, and Mars, and are composed primarily of rock. Outer planets, further from the sun, are Jupiter, Saturn, Uranus and Neptune. Saturn is surrounded by a phenomenal set of brilliant rings. The outer planets are not formed from rock but, rather, are huge gaseous bodies. All planets, other than the Earth, have several to multiple moons.

Planets being nearer the sun have warmer surface temperatures than those that are further away. Jupiter has very strong gravitational attractions while lesser forces are present on Saturn, Uranus, and Neptune. The planets travel at different orbital speeds, accelerating as they get nearer the sun. Astronomers believe there may be several additional undiscovered planets far beyond current areas of exploration. Although a mystery, only God knows what other heavenly bodies are yet undetected.

SEASONS, DAYS, AND YEARS

Creation of the solar system has direct bearing on the seasons, days, and years. The four seasons are caused by the 23.5 degree rotation of the Earth at its axis, giving the surface an ecliptic rather than perpendicular plane. This angler plane on the Earth's surface exposes the northern and southern hemispheres to the sun at different times. The tilted surface allows the rays of the sun to strike the Earth at a more direct angle during the summer season in both hemispheres, producing warmer temperatures. During winter seasons, the Earth's tilt results in the rays of the sun hitting the planet at extreme angles, plus the slight incline also causes shorter days.

A solar or ordinary day is defined as the time required for the Earth to rotate once on its axis. The length of a solar day varies slightly during the year; however, to avoid confusion, the average time for each day has been established as 24 hours. Astronomers use the sidereal day which is actually four minutes shorter that a solar day. This minimal time difference results from the tilt of the Earth's rotation, which also causes day and night lengths to vary during the year.

A year is specified as the time required for the Earth to complete one orbit around the sun. Known as the solar or tropical year, the time needed for this to occur is 365 days, five hours, 48 minutes and 46 seconds. Calendar years consist of 365 days but are adjusted to 366 days every four years, allowing for the small additional rotational time periods. The sun is used for quick daily measurements of time, but the stars are viewed to determine precise times. It is possible to calculate exact times for sunrise, sunset, moonrise, and moonset for most major cities in the United States by knowing their latitudes and longitudes.

In summary, the axis of the Earth is tilted producing the four seasons as different parts are oriented toward the sun at various times of the year. The surface of the Earth moves at 24,855 miles every 24 hours or at a speed of about 1,035 miles per hour at the level of the equator. Of course, the speed reduces to almost zero at either of the Earth's poles. It requires 23.93 hours for the Earth to rotate daily on its axis; this is a sidereal day. While the Earth orbits on its axis once a day, it also rotates around the sun annually, every 365.26 days.

Once more, the creative acts of day four are nearly impossible to comprehend by the human mind. Not only did God create a gigantic sun with various lighting and energy-generating capabilities for use by the entire universe, but He further flung multiple billions of additional complex objects into space, located considerably beyond our realm of vision or mental comprehension.

After day four, there are now seasons that meet the growth and reproductive needs of plants and future animals. Regulated precise days, months, and years have been established. Dark nights permit rest and revitalization of plant life, thus providing needed food for animals.

What will be next on God's creative agenda? Obviously, the Earth is ready for living animals to enter the picture. A daily energized source of light is available to foster plant growth and replication, providing food and nesting sites for animals. Light-dark cycles will meet the needs of hormonal reproductive interactions within animals and man. These cycles will also allow diurnal (day living) and nocturnal (night living) animals to survive comfortably. It surely appears that God's creation plan remains on track.

> *"When I look at your heavens, the work of your fingers, the moon and the stars, which you have set in place, what is man that you are mindful of him, and the son of man that you care for him?"* (Psalm 8:3-4).

Chapter 5

Day Five—Sea Creatures, Birds, and Insects

"And God said, Let the waters swarm with swarms of living creatures, and let birds fly above the Earth across the expanse of the heavens. So God created the great sea creatures and every living creature that moves, with which the waters swarm, according to their kinds, and every winged bird according to its kind. And God saw that it was good. And God blessed them, saying, Be fruitful and multiply and fill the waters in the seas, and let birds multiply on the Earth. And there was evening and there was morning, the fifth day" (Gen 1:20-23).

Now that light, air, water, and food are available, the Earth was prepared for creation of animal life. The first full day of sunshine, an established season, an outlined day, and a defined time would greet the new creations. The total number of sea, air, and earth-dwelling animals is unknown. Estimates vary from two million to over 100 million, with the best estimate somewhere near 10 million. On day five, God created sea creatures and birds. Although the day for creation of insects is not mentioned in Genesis, many biblical scholars believe that insects were also part of the day five creation events. However, there are some who place creation of insects on the sixth day. Since the great majority fly (over 85%), insects do not fit well into the "creeping things" category stated for day six creation activities. The simultaneous appearance of insects with other flying animals seems more tenable, so they will be included in this day five creation chapter.

SEA CREATURES

Genesis 1:20 indicates that great swarms of sea creatures were created. Certainly, the Earth's massive oceans, lakes, rivers, streams, and ponds could accommodate large numbers of these animals. It has been estimated that the extent and depth of the oceans encompass 99% of the Earth's living space and provides a habitat for 21,000 species of sea animals. In Genesis 1:22, scripture states clearly that the swarms of sea animals were created according to their *kind*. The word *kind* appears ten times in Genesis 1. The Hebrew word for *kind* is *min* and should not be confused with species, a term used by current-day biologists. The word *kind* is much broader and may include several species. Crossbreeding among species is possible, in fact, quite common as seen in the canine family. Different canine species such as dogs, wolves, and coyotes will crossbreed but remain part of their created *kind*. Similar crossbreeding occurs in the equine *kind*. Horses, donkeys, and mules are different species but retain their *kind* designation. Thus, the argument that animals (*kinds*) undergo evolutionary changes is false and invalid.

There is great diversity among water-dwelling animals which includes the smallest to the largest of all known species. Sea mammals are among the largest ocean animals consisting of whales, dolphins, porpoises, seals, walruses, dugongs, and manatees. Many brightly colored fish, lobsters, and sea urchins live among tropical coral reefs. Hundreds of additional fish species live throughout the world's salt or fresh water bodies. Anemones, barnacles, mussels, octopuses, and starfish live in shallow water and on rocks. Some sea creatures, such as clams and anglerfish, live in the deep, dark, cold parts of the oceans.

Many interesting facts are known about sea animals. The largest animal living in the ocean is the blue whale, reaching up to 100 feet in length and weighing around 120 tons. These animals are larger than others anywhere in the world and even surpass the size of the former dinosaurs. The killer whale swims at 34 miles per hour making it the fastest sea animal. Some rare deep-sea fish possess both female and male sex organs, and other species are able to change their sex over their life spans.

Unique feeding methods are used by the different sea creatures. Barnacles sweep water past their living habitats and strain out tiny plankton (microscopic animals and plants) for food. Some whales are filter feeders, gulping large mouthfuls of water that contain small fish and other marine organisms and, afterwards, filtering this food-laden water through their body's strainers called baleen. Next, the captured food is swallowed with some whales eating up to four tons daily. Most sea creatures obtain oxygen by removing it from water pumped across their gills, but a few species absorb oxygen through their skins.

BIRDS

Birds are defined as warm-blooded, winged, egg-laying, feathered vertebrates. Although 115 species are known to have become extinct, ornithologists have identified over 9,700 kinds of currently living birds. In addition to lungs, birds have air sacs in their bones and bodies, plus lightweight feathers instead of heavy coats, all of which decrease their weights. Equipped with bills, rather than heavy jaws and teeth, further lightens their bodies. They have fairly large brains, keen eyesight and hearing, but a poor sense of smell. The beak of each species is adapted for specific feeding habits like collecting nectar, scooping up fish, breaking hard seeds, catching insects, or drilling into plants for food or construction of nesting sites.

Birds are of considerable value in eliminating insect pests, feeding on weed seeds, and ingesting carrion (dead animals). Domestic fowl provide eggs and meat for human consumption as well as feathers for decorative projects. Game species are used for sport and food while other birds are maintained as pets. A few bird species have been used to transmit messages during wartime. There is one known poisonous bird, the pitted pitohui, which lives in New Guinea. The poison on its feathers and skin provides protection against predators.

The bee hummingbird is the smallest known bird measuring only two inches in length. Ostriches are the largest birds, reaching up to 350 pounds in weight. The largest flying bird is the Kori Bustard of Africa that weighs up to 42 pounds. The Andean Condor is reported to have the greatest wingspan, extending to 10 feet.

Interesting habits are observed in different birds. Hummingbirds can fly straight up and backwards. Golden eagles fly at great heights, often above mountain peaks. A few birds such as penguins and ostriches are unable to fly. The fastest of all animals is the peregrine falcon, reaching speeds of more than 200 miles per hour while swooping down on prey.

Feather renewal or molting is triggered by changes in photoperiods. During this time the entire plumage, including flight and tail feathers, is completely replaced as damaged feathers need to be renewed. This feather-renewal process is species dependent, but usually occurs after the breeding season when the young need little or no care. While molting, fat is also deposited and stored in the body.

Birds sing mainly during the spring season and the male does most of the vocalizing, again triggered by changes in day length. For centuries, Japanese bird fanciers have practiced the art of yogai in which caged birds are forced to sing in midwinter by lengthening their days, using candlelight for three or four hours after sunset. By increasing light exposure periods, Dutch hunters have stimulated various finches to sing prematurely in October for the purpose of enticing autumn migrating finches into traps. Egg production may be increased by lengthening periods of light. More than 200 years ago, Spaniards were providing artificial illumination at night for this purpose, a common practice continued in the poultry industry today. Changes in photoperiod are also used to improve breeding success in pet birds, resulting in the production of additional young.

Many birds migrate for long distances to find better feeding and nesting sites. After the breeding season, they return to their southern habitats where winter temperatures and living conditions are more favorable. Some migrating birds have what has been described as an internal magnetic compass. This navigational aid is driven by the Earth's magnetic field. Homing pigeons also seem to use tiny variations in the Earth's magnetic field to find their way home.

INSECTS

Insects are animals that have three body parts (head, thorax, abdomen), six jointed legs, two antennae, and an exoskeleton (external skeleton). Entomologists believe that there are approximately one million insect species living throughout the world; in fact, it has been conjectured that 50 to 95% of the world's living animals are insects. Insects eat more plants than all other animals combined and process plant and animal refuse for enriching soil.

Body structure of insects is quite simple; blood and other body fluids flow around rather freely inside their exoskeletons, breathing tubes supply oxygen, and their digestive systems consist of long tubes. An insect's nervous system is fairly refined and ensures good sight, smell, taste, hearing, and touch perceptions. Essentially, all insects reproduce sexually through mating of males and females. Most lay eggs but a few produce live births following internal hatching of their eggs. Generally, newly hatched insects begin life in areas where their required foods are plentiful. Some insects are cold-blooded so their optimum growth depends upon appropriate environmental temperatures.

Numerous useful products are produced by insects including honey, silk, and wax, and they are the principal animals that pollinate plants. Insects also provide an abundant source of food for other animals, especially birds and fish. Feeding on insects is facilitated since nocturnal animals have rhythms that are diametrically out of phase with diurnal animals. Whether diurnal, nocturnal, or crepuscular (active at twilight or just before dawn), all animals appear to have the ability to anticipate the coming sunset and sunrise and, thus, appear in the right place at the right time to feed on other animals. For example, as moths and flying insects come out at night, so do their predators such as bats and owls.

Some animals created on day five may cause injury or death to humans. The box jellyfish, or sea wasp, is one of the deadliest stinging sea animals known, having killed numbers of people. The Portuguese man-of-war, another jellyfish, inflicts severe stinging injuries; however, the stings are seldom fatal. Both of these jellyfish are found around the coasts of Australia. The blue-ringed octopus, also living in Australian waters, either bites or squirts poisonous venom into surrounding waters, killing other sea animals or people. Sharks often wound people and occasionally kill and eat them. Flocks of large birds have been known to cause aircraft to crash. Several insects sting, bite, or transmit serious diseases and a few cause major damage to vegetative plants and building structures. In addition, various parasites may invade the bodies of humans and animals causing serious debilitating illnesses.

God does not waste his resources. After creating the Earth, bodies of water, and the atmosphere, he placed uniquely and wonderfully designed animals into each separate environment. Great swarms, flocks, and masses of animals of various anatomic and physiologic makeup were placed precisely where they could survive and multiply. Hardly the result of evolutionary chance and good luck!

Day six of creation is now on the horizon. Large areas on the Earth's surface remain available to support additional living creatures. Hang on, the greatest creative acts are about to occur.

> *"Lord, you have been our dwelling place in all generations.*
> *Before the mountains were brought forth, or ever you had*
> *formed the Earth and the world, from everlasting to*
> *everlasting you are God"* (Psalm 90:1).

Chapter 6

Day Six—Livestock, Creeping Things, Beasts, and Man

"And God said, Let the Earth bring forth living creatures according to their kinds—livestock and creeping things and beasts of the Earth according to their kinds. And it was so. And God made the beasts of the Earth according to their kinds and the livestock according to their kinds, and everything that creeps on the ground according to its kind. And God saw that it was good. Then God said, Let us make man in our image, after our likeness. And let them have dominion over the fish of the sea and over the birds of the heavens and over the livestock and over all the Earth and over every creeping thing that creeps on the Earth. So God created man in his own image, in the image of God he created him; male and female he created them. And God blessed them. And God said to them, Be fruitful and multiply and fill the Earth and subdue it and have dominion over the fish of the sea and over the birds of the heavens and over every living thing that moves on the Earth" (Genesis 1:24-28).

On the final day of creation, God ended his activities with His ultimate goal: to create man. Prior to this last act, He created several groups of animals. The categories of animals mentioned as created on day six include livestock, beasts, and creeping things. It is generally accepted that the designation of livestock includes mammals commonly found on farms today plus other domesticated species. Beasts are thought to be the mammals currently considered as being in the wild kingdom. These two categories of mammals number about 4,500 currently known species. Mammals are warm-blooded, four-legged, vertebrate, milk-producing animals (with exception bats and some sea animals). Although mammals are not the predominant group of animals on the Earth, they are the ones seen most and those with which man interacts primarily. Creeping things include amphibians and reptiles plus other animals that remain closely associated with the ground.

Mentioned previously in this chapter, verse 24 in Genesis 1 reveals that animals and man were brought forth from the Earth. Being made from the Earth, they will also return to the Earth after death. King Solomon describes the end of life in animals and man, "All go to one place. All are from the dust, and to dust all return" (Ecclesiastes 2:20). Animals were tame creatures originally and they were plant-ingesting vegetarians. "And to every beast of the Earth and to every bird of the heavens and to everything that creeps on the Earth, everything that has the breath of life, I have given every green plant for food. And it was so" (Genesis 1:30). God provided a useful interactive benefit between plant and animal life. Plants use carbon dioxide and produce oxygen during photosynthesis, while animals inhale oxygen and expire carbon dioxide during respiration, thus providing an environmental balance in these life-sustaining gasses.

LIVESTOCK

Livestock includes animals which are quite familiar to everyone such as horses, cattle, sheep, goats, swine, and various pet species. Diversity is obvious in these mammals as some have simple (single) stomachs while cattle have a four-compartment paunch. They have single or cloven hooves, light to heavy hair coverings, or wool coats. The different mammals may have a few or many mammary glands, and they vary greatly in behaviors and intelligence levels. Horses have a complex stay apparatus in which their legs become locked in place allowing them to remain standing while sleeping.

Although man was originally instructed to refrain from using these animals for food, they surely must have provided considerable joy and companionship. Even today, dogs are still known as "man's best friend." Mammals are very valuable animals since we now use them for food, clothing, medical research, companionship, transportation, work, sport, hunting, protection, entertainment, and clothing.

Previous creation of the sun provides great benefits in managing some livestock. Farmers and country folk have known about the effects of day length for centuries and have used changes in light periods for commercial advantage. Cows exposed to light for 16-18 hours a day increase their milk yield in general by eight to 10 per cent due to longer periods of illumination. Providing 15 to 16 hours of extended daylight to horses causes the breeding season (estrus) in mares to move ahead to an earlier time during the year, thus advancing the birth of young by several months. These longer light exposures also cause shedding of winter hair coats and regrowth of short and shiny hair, which is desirable for early participation of horses in shows. However, premature growth of short hair may endanger horses by exposing them to cold late winter temperatures, so measures must be taken to protect them from inclement weather.

CREEPING THINGS (Amphibians and Reptiles)

As stated previously, some creationist scholars place the introduction of insects in the group of creeping things. The author of this book believes they should be included as day five creations since over 85% of them fly, and would fit better with the appearance of other flying animals.

More than 5,500 amphibian species live throughout the world except in the Antarctica region. These animals include frogs, toads, salamanders, and newts. They are cold-blooded and hatch from eggs to begin their lives in water as gill-breathers without legs. After metamorphosis from a larval state, most amphibians grow four legs and become partly terrestrial (land-living) and mature as air-breathers having developed lungs. Most species have no scales and breathe and absorb water through their skins. Despite their need for water, many are found living in desert areas.

Amphibians rarely cause injury since they would rather avoid than confront people. They are often used for scientific and medical research. Amphibians have fairly specialized light, humidity, and heat requirements so they should not be kept as pets.

Reptiles comprise approximately 6,000 species of air-breathing vertebrates having skin covered with scales or plates. Snakes, lizards, turtles, tortoises, and crocodilians (alligators and crocodiles) are all reptiles. Although reptiles breathe through their lungs, a few can also absorb oxygen from water through membranes in their mouths. All of them are cold-blooded and have four, two, or no legs.

Snakes and lizards comprise most of the reptiles. Snakes do not have legs, hearing capabilities, nor moveable eyelids. Since they are able to disarticulate their jaws, they can swallow prey up to three times the diameter of their bodies. Snakes are the world's most efficient controllers of wild rodent populations. Poisonous species may bite and produce serious tissue damage and, sometimes death.

Lizards have four legs and long tails which they can shed during escape from predators and, thereafter, grow new tails. Turtles differ from other reptiles in that their shells are part of their skeletons and serve as strong protective coverings. Turtles travel at the slowest speed of all animals moving at about 0.10 mile per hour. Green turtles have been known to migrate more than 1,400 miles to lay their eggs. Turtles have been found that lived for over 100 years with a record age of 200 years.

Crocodiles and alligators are the largest reptiles, walking on land with webbed feet and using their tails for swimming. They have strong jaws and teeth that tear apart prey they capture on land or in the water and, occasionally, crocodilians attack, injure, or kill people. The largest reptile known is the saltwater crocodile which grows up to 23 feet in length.

BEASTS (Wildlife)

When created originally, wild mammals were tame and friendly. Thus, describing them in today's vernacular may not portray them accurately as they first appeared on earth. Because only current activities and behaviors of these animals are known, they will be described as they appear now. Christians eagerly anticipate the day when these animals will again be sociable creatures during the millennial period. "The wolf shall dwell with the lamb, and the leopard shall lie down with the young goat, and the calf and the lion and the fattened calf together; and a little child shall lead them. The cow and the bear shall graze; their young shall lie down together; and the lion shall eat straw like the ox. The nursing child shall play over the hole of the cobra, and the weaned child shall put his hand on the adder's den" (Isaiah 11: 6-9).

Wild mammals are found worldwide in the grasslands, polar regions, tropics, mountains, deserts, and rain forests. Since there are numerous wild animals of vast diversity, it would be impossible to describe these mammals in depth in this book. A visit to a zoo or wildlife park would be of value to anyone wishing to gain additional information about these animals. Wild species range from tiny field mice to large elephants, each having specific anatomic and physiologic features, habits, and behaviors, as well as food and environmental requirements.

Many wild mammals are highly secretive and prefer to avoid contact with humans. Sometimes, when accidental contact does occur, wild animals become defensive and aggressive and, out of fear, they may injure man. Generally, attacks from bears, the large cat species, wild canids and many other wild mammals result when the animals are protecting their young, their territories are invaded, or surprise contacts from outsiders take place.

Information about wild animal groups is quite interesting and a few examples are provided. Marsupials make up a unique array of animals that include kangaroos, wallabies, wombats, opossums, and several other lesser known species. These mammals have abdominal pouches into which infants crawl immediately after birth. Following short gestation periods, newborn marsupials arrive in an immature state and further development occurs in the pouches. They nurse from nipples within the pouches and remain there until they can function in the outside world. Most species of marsupials are found in Australia; however, they also live in New Guinea, and North, South and Central America. They are primarily nocturnal with highly efficient senses of smell and hearing.

One of the more fascinating wild animal species is the bat. This winged mammal lives in all parts of the world but is most numerous in the tropics. Bats have a mouse-like appearance with soft fine fur, and their ears are generally large compared to the rest of their bodies. Some bats exist under solitary conditions while others prefer large communal living arrangements. While resting, they hang with their heads downward while clinging to a perch or crevice. Bats are primarily insect-feeders; however, a few species eat fruit, small fish, or immature frogs. These flying mammals are of great economic value because they destroy massive numbers of insects. A single bat has been reported to eat 1,200 small insects during a half hour period. The longest life span listed for a bat is 32 years. Essentially, all bats are nocturnal and they use echolocation (sonar) for direction during flight. They emit high-pitched sounds which return to them via echos, thus identifying the locations and sizes of insects and objects. Bats in the northern hemisphere migrate or hibernate during cold weather. They are relatively free from diseases, but occasionally one may transmit rabies to another animal or to a human.

Following are some fascinating facts about wild mammals. Camels endure hot climates and have water storage reservoirs in their humps. The cheetah has been identified as the animal that can run at the highest speed, 70 miles per hour. The tallest mammal is the giraffe, reaching up to 20 feet in height, while the smallest is the 1.3 inch-long Kitli's hognosed bat from Thailand, weighing only 0.07 ounce. The Rhinoceros has the heaviest skin of all mammals, measuring up to one inch in thickness.

MAN

Following the creation of man, God took a rib from him and created a woman. "And the rib that the Lord had taken from the man he made into a woman and brought her to the man" (Genesis 2:22). Thus, after the initial creation of Adam, the term *man* in scripture should always be considered to include both men and women. The creation of man was the end point of God's creative activities. Man was a distinct creation who was destined originally to live forever. God changed this dictum after man sinned by eating the forbidden fruit in the Garden of Eden and He decreed that man would die. "And the Lord commanded the man saying, You may surely eat of every tree of the garden, but of the tree of the knowledge of good and evil you shall not eat, for in the day that you eat of it you shall surely die" (Genesis 2:16-17). Regardless of man's fall, he was God's ultimate creation, not merely another member of the animal kingdom as purported by many of today's evolutionists.

In Genesis 1:26, God said, "Let us make man in our image, after our likeness," which indicates the trinity was involved. He likely did not create man in an analogous bodily form because, "God is spirit, and those who worship Him must worship in spirit and truth" (John 4:24). God created man with a spiritual, natural, and moral likeness, one who could comprehend and show love, appreciate beauty, enjoy fellowship, and obey and worship his creator. Man would think conceptually, make moral decisions, express emotions, use speech communication, and possess an eternal soul that would endure forever.

Unlike God's previous creations, man was a highly organized being incorporating complicated physiological, chemical, and anatomical features. The Psalmist, David, expressed the marvel of man's creation. "For you formed my inward parts; you knitted me together in my mother's womb. I praise you, for I am fearfully and wonderfully made. Wonderful are your works; my soul knows it very well. My frame was not hidden from you, when I was being made in secret, intricately woven in the depths of the Earth" (Psalm 139:13-15).

Numerous books have been written describing the intricacies and splendor of man's created body so only a very superficial review will be presented. The body consists of ten major systems, all of which must work together in a precise manner to ensure health and happiness. Some body organs serve as part of multiple systems in order to accomplish required body functions. The *integumentary system* consists of the skin, hair, nails, sweat glands, and sebaceous (oil) glands. Adipose (fat) tissue is deposited just beneath the skin and around some internal organs, and provides fuel reserves and insulation for the body. As the largest organ of the body, the skin provides a protective covering and is the sensory link to man's environment. A combination of the brain, spinal cord, and a large network of nerves makes up the *nervous system*. The brain is involved in thought processes, emotional responses, sensory detection, and communication. The special senses of vision, smell, taste, hearing, and touch are all activated through the nervous system. A necessary component of the body is the *circulatory system* which includes the heart and blood vessels. The heart pumps blood throughout the body to transfer oxygen, nutrients, immune cells, hormones, and waste components. Blood cells include erythrocytes (red blood cells) which carry oxygen to every part of the body, leucocytes (white blood cells) that fight infection and foreign materials, and platelets which are involved in blood clotting and wound healing.

The *respiratory system* consists of the nose, nasopharynx, trachea, and lungs. This system inspires external supplies of oxygen into the body and expires carbon dioxide and water back into the outside atmosphere. Ingestion and processing of food are accomplished by the *gastrointestinal system*, where nutrients are converted into usable components, and thereafter, distributed to all body tissues via the circulatory system. This system also removes wastes from the body. The *musculoskeletal system* includes the skeleton with its attached ligaments, tendons, and cartilage plus the body's muscles. The skeleton provides structural strength for the body and facilitates movement. Marrow inside the bones produces red blood cells and serves as the site for storage of calcium and phosphate. The gonads (ovaries and testes) and associated female and male sex organs make up the *reproductive system*. Fertilization and fetal development occur through the reproductive system.

A highly developed component of the body is the *endocrine system* which consists of several glands including the pituitary, thyroid, parathyroids, adrenals, pancreas, and gonads. These glands produce hormones that are transported by the blood vessels to various systems in the body, causing required responses or actions where targeted. The *urinary system* includes the kidneys, ureters, bladder, and urethra. These organs function to remove and excrete excess water and wastes from the blood in the form of urine. White blood cells, the thymus gland, lymph nodes, and lymph channels make up the *immune system*. This system identifies and destroys or nullifies foreign materials in the body through interactions with antibodies (special neutralizing proteins from white blood cells).

It is no small miracle that all of the body's systems work in harmony 24 hours every day to provide optimal human health. Occasionally, if one system weakens or becomes partially dysfunctional, another system may be able to compensate partially to maintain relatively normal daily activities. It is abundantly obvious that millions of years of evolutionary changes would never have produced the highly coordinated functions performed by the body's many efficient systems.

God's principal goal was to have man inhabit the Earth and maintain dominion over all He had created. "You have given him dominion over the works of your hands; you have put all things under his feet, all sheep and oxen, and also the beasts of the field, the birds of the heavens, and the fish of the sea, whatever passes along the paths of the seas" (Psalm 8:6-8). Part of this command involved naming the newly created animals. "So out of the ground the Lord God formed every beast of the field and every bird of the heavens and brought them to the man to see what he would call them. And whatever the man called every living creature, that was its name" (Genesis 2:19). Further, man was to be fruitful, multiply, and fill the Earth. With the current world population, it appears that this command has been fulfilled.

God surely loved man because, rather than speaking a garden into existence as He had done with the masses of previous plants, He personally planted a magnificent garden for Adam. "And the Lord God planted a garden in Eden, in the east, and there he put the man whom he had formed" (Genesis 2:8). As demanded for animals originally, man was also to live as a vegetarian. "And God said, Behold I have given you every plant yielding seed that is on the face of all the Earth, and every tree with seed in its fruit. You shall have them for food" (Genesis 1:29). According to this verse it appears that, in addition to the Garden of Eden, Adam also had access to all the other plants on the Earth. However, as noted previously, God provided specific instructions which forbade eating the fruit from one tree.

As a vegetarian, Adam would refrain from killing animals; however, after Adam's sin, animals were sacrificed in worshiping God. "In the course of time Cain brought to the Lord an offering of the fruit of the ground, and Abel also brought of the firstborn of his flock and of their fat portions. And the Lord had regard for Abel and his offering" (Genesis 4:3-4). It was not until after the Noahic flood that man was allowed to use animals for food. "Every moving thing that lives shall be food for you. And as I gave you the green plants, I give you everything" (Genesis 9:3).

On day six of creation, God designed animals that were more complex than the aquatic, air, and insect species created on the prior day. Finally, He formed His ultimate creation, man, from the dust of the Earth. Following His previous creations, God reviewed His actions each day and said it was good. After creating man He said everything was *very* good. He had filled all the voids in his universe according to His satisfaction. What an incredible record we have in Genesis, portraying divine creation by an all-knowing, omnipotent and caring God. His marvelous creative work is now completed and He will rest from his busy and magnificent week of activity.

> *"And God saw everything that he had made, and behold, it was very good. And there was evening and there was morning, the sixth day"* (Genesis 1:31).

Chapter 7

Day Seven—God Rests

"Thus the heavens and the Earth were finished, and all the host of them. And on the seventh day God finished his work that he had done, and he rested on the seventh day from all his work that he had done. So God blessed the seventh day and made it holy, because on it God rested from all his work that he had done in creation" (Genesis 2:1-3).

God had finished His colossal creation over a six-day period. He now states that He rested on the seventh day. A question may be asked, "Was God weary and did He need rest?" Certainly not! So, why is this declaration in the Bible? This statement was likely included in scripture because God wanted to ensure that people rest but, more importantly, He wants His people to know that a day should be set aside each week for special worship.

The seventh day during which God rested was known as the Sabbath. The word Sabbath means cessation or perfect rest from activity. This was the Jewish day of rest; however, Christians have taken the first day of the week, Sunday, as their day of rest, which has also been designated as the Lord's Day. This day was selected since, following His crucifixion, Christ arose from the dead on the first day of the week. At a later time, the apostle Paul was in the upper room serving communion to his disciples on the first day of the week. "On the first day of the week, when we were gathered together to break bread, Paul talked with them, intending to depart on the next day, and he prolonged his speech until midnight" (Acts 20:7). God originally created the heavens and the Earth and, on resurrection day, God instituted the new creation through which all the sins of His born-again children were placed under the blood of His Son, Jesus Christ.

God commanded six days of work and, thereafter, one day of rest for mankind. Whether observing the Sabbath or Sunday (the Lord's Day), God expects one-seventh of a person's time to be reserved for Him. We are not left uninformed regarding what God wants from people on their day of rest. He clearly instructs that it is to be a holy day. "Observe the Sabbath day, to keep it holy, as the LORD your God commanded you. Six days you shall labor and do all your work, but the seventh day is a Sabbath to the LORD your God. On it you shall not do any work, you or your son or your daughter or your male servant or your female servant, or your ox or your donkey or any of your livestock, or the sojourner who is within your gates, that your male servant and your female servant may rest as well as you" (Deut. 5:12-14). The mandate is to keep the day of rest holy. No doubt, most people have their own ideas concerning what keeping the day holy involves. God blessed the seventh day and He expects man to worship and fellowship with Him.

An additional command requires that we assemble with other Christians as practiced in current-day church attendance, and God encourages us to love each other and to do good deeds. "And let us consider how to stir up one another to love and good works, not neglecting to meet together, as is the habit of some, but encouraging one another, and all the more as you see the day drawing near" (Hebrews 10:24-25). Whatever one does to keep the Lord's Day holy, it appears that Sunday worship with other Christians is essential. Other Lord's Day activities in which Christians are involved frequently include visiting with family members, encouraging others (shut-ins, sick, homeless, prisoners), comforting those who grieve, writing encouraging notes, babysitting for those who need some rest, sharing food and material things with those less fortunate, enjoying God's creation, and telling others of the saving grace of Jesus. Surely there are additional holy activities, too numerous to specify, which would be appropriate to practice on Sundays. Ultimately, suitable holy activities to be undertaken on the Lord's Day will be determined by each individual according to her or his understanding of scripture.

For those who hold to dispensationalism, that there is an age for every biblical period, those living now are in the "age of grace" which loosens the hold of the Mosaic law on people's daily lives. It is no longer necessary to be bound by the law which was given to the nation Israel to separate them from the pagan nations around them. Although the law is still applicable to Christians' lives, it is not the rule of life.

Equally important in deciding which activities are appropriate on the weekly day of rest is determining what types of work should be avoided. Several thoughts about this matter prevail and are occasionally practiced. Some homemakers believe that preparing meals and washing dishes on Sundays are improper. There are those who believe the use of tractors or other farm equipment on the Lord's Day should be avoided, even if such activities would actually reduce animal care and feeding workloads during that day. Further, incidents have been reported where people have refused to perform work required to protect their property, animals, crops, vegetables, or flowers from freezing, flooding, or other perils on Sundays.

Specific instructions for right or wrong work activities on the Lord's Day are generally missing in scripture. However, it appears that those work-related jobs that could be done on other days of the week should not be performed on Sundays. Moses gave an example of this in the gathering of manna by the Israelites. They were to avoid collecting this food on the Sabbath but, rather, were to garner sufficient quantities on the prior day. "On the sixth day they gathered twice as much bread, two omers each. And when all the leaders of the congregation came and told Moses, he said to them, This is what the LORD has commanded: Tomorrow is a day of solemn rest, a holy Sabbath to the LORD; bake what you will bake and boil what you will boil, and all that is left over lay aside to be kept till the morning. So they laid it aside till the morning, as Moses commanded them, and it did not stink, and there were no worms in it. Moses said, Eat it today, for today is a Sabbath to the LORD; today you will not find it in the field. Six days you shall gather it, but on the seventh day, which is a Sabbath, there will be none. On the seventh day some of the people went out to gather, but they found none" (Exodus 16:22-27).

In Jesus' day, restoring the health of a person, although involving work, was performed on the Sabbath. He obviously considered healing of the sick an appropriate activity. "Now he was teaching in one of the synagogues on the Sabbath. And there was a woman who had a disabling spirit for eighteen years. She was bent over and could not fully straighten herself. When Jesus saw her, he called her over and said to her, Woman, you are freed from your disability. And he laid His hands on her, and immediately she was made straight, and she glorified God. But the ruler of the synagogue, indignant because Jesus had healed on the Sabbath, said to the people, There are six days in which work ought to be done. Come on those days and be healed, and not on the Sabbath day. Then the Lord answered him, You hypocrites! Does not each of you on the Sabbath untie his ox or his donkey from the manger and lead it away to water it?" (Luke 13:10-15).

Rescuing a child or animal in danger was an approved Lord's Day function. "And he said to them, Which of you, having a son or an ox that has fallen into a well on a Sabbath day, will not immediately pull him out" (Luke 14:5). Essentially, every individual has been endowed with a level of common sense, some more than others, to make Sunday's work decisions as believed prudent. Unfortunately, Christians sometimes have interesting discussions about the activities performed by others on Sundays, and may be quick to judge their circumstances and motives. God is not pleased with such judgement and condemnation and we are told, "Judge not, and you will not be judged; condemn not, and you will not be condemned; forgive and you will be forgiven" (Luke 6:37). Only God will ultimately determine what work was or was not appropriate on Sundays, and He will set the record straight when Christ returns for His children.

It is interesting that God addresses those who refuse to work. He expects those who are well and able-bodied to labor a full work week. Even the first man created, Adam, had to work in the beautiful garden God provided. "The Lord God took the man and put him in the garden

60

of Eden to work it and keep it" (Genesis 2:15). Jesus displayed his work ethic by laboring in Joseph's carpenter shop. One of the ten commandments given to Moses on Mount Sinai reiterates God's requirement that man should work. "Six days you shall labor, and do all your work" (Exodus 20:9).

Verses from the book of Proverbs that are quoted frequently suggest that work habits of the lowly ant should be an inspirational role model for human beings. "Go to the ant, O sluggard; consider her ways, and be wise. Without having any chief, officer, or ruler, she prepares her bread in summer and gathers her food in harvest. How long will you lie there, O sluggard? When will you arise from your sleep?" (Proverbs 6:6-9). God provides a stern rebuke to those who do not work, advocating they not be allowed to eat. "For even when we were with you, we would give you this command: If anyone is not willing to work, let him not eat" (2 Thessalonians 3:10). In addition to this reference about laziness, anyone who does not support his family is rebuked strongly. "But if anyone does not provide for his relatives, and especially for members of his household, he has denied the faith and is worse than an unbeliever" (1 Timothy 5:8).

God rested on the seventh day as should all humankind. From personal understanding of scripture, decisions can be made regarding what activities may be pursued on the Lord's Day as well as the categories of work that appear to be appropriate or unseemly. Christians should appreciate their God-given abilities and talents to perform work. Those involved in the working world have an excellent opportunity to present a witness to those outside of Christ; He needs dedicated Christians in all walks of life. Finally, God is not pleased with those who are able to work but refuse to do so. Anyone who can work but elects to live on welfare, or with financial assistance from other social programs, violates the principles of scripture.

> *"Come to me, all who labor and are heavy laden, and I will give you rest. Take my yoke upon you, and learn from me, for I am gentle and lowly in heart, and you will find rest for your souls"* (Matthew 11:28-29).

Chapter 8

How Big Is Your God?

"Now faith is the assurance of things hoped for, the conviction of things not seen. For by it the people of old received their commendation. By faith we understand that the universe was created by the word of God, so that what is seen was not made out of things that are visible" (Hebrews 11: 1-3).

In the beginning, in six literal 24-hour days, God created everything from nothing (*ex nihilo*). No big bang, no gaps, no continuing false and fabricated evolutionary theories, but simply, *Elohim*, the omnipotent God created! The entire created universe remains unified through intricate binding forces produced by positively and negatively charged atoms. Massive bodies of water are held in place by an unseen force. Multiple thousands of plants and animals reproduce and thrive under unique symbiotic arrangements. Millions of small to immense heavenly bodies remain in their defined orbits.

Creation of new matter and life has ceased; however, crossbreeding among animal kinds does occur and some plants are changed by grafting, genetic manipulation, or exposure to altered environments. Although this information is known by many evolutionists, they choose to remain blinded and deny or suppress God's magnificent and orderly creative acts. They refuse to accept the fact that there has never been, nor will there ever be, a single disagreement between accurate proven scientific findings and the Bible.

Numerous wonders are found in all inanimate and living created things. This chapter provides additional interesting facts about God's greatness as demonstrated by His marvelous creation. Everything that God made was declared as either good or very good. It would be impossible to improve on that kind of creation.

The first Model T Ford was built in 1908. Ford Motor Company personnel updated their automobiles and all subsequent models every year since then and, frequently, made additional minor to major changes between model years. We should be relieved that neither an automobile nor any other manufacturing company was responsible for creation. In the beginning, God created all living things, including man, and he continues to replicate his original models without change. He obviously got it right the first time. Isn't that the kind of God we want?

Interestingly, evolutionists claim that birds evolved from reptiles. Not exactly a brilliant conclusion since reptiles arrived a day later on day six rather than day five. The platypus is a good example of God's finished creative work and, possibly, a portrayal of his sense of humor. This mammal nurses its young with milk, has a bill like a duck, and lays eggs. The platypus remains an enigma to evolutionists. Although the platypus appears to be in a state of evolutionary transition, each newly hatched baby is exactly like its parent, even after thousands of years.

God endowed many animals with capabilities to adapt to different environmental conditions. Desert animals have been created with high heat and low humidity tolerances. Some such as centipedes, kangaroo rats, rattlesnakes, and scorpions stay in underground burrows during hot weather, returning during cooler nights to find food and water. Several desert animals, including turtles, and lizards, have special body features which help them adjust to high temperatures. Ground squirrels, mice, lizards, frogs, and snails go into a deep sleep (estivation) to escape hot weather. Other animals have light-colored skins that reflect sunlight or they may have long ears that facilitate dissipation of heat. In contrast, polar-living animals have heavy fur coats, short ears, and small tails to prevent heat loss.

Self-preservation is another innate behavior found in animals. They may find hiding sites, come out only during the day or night when their natural enemies are absent, camouflage themselves to blend into their surroundings, change skin colors, mimic other animals or plants, fly away, play dead, fight, use protective armor, or emit foul-smelling chemical secretions.

God equipped animals well for moving to the best locations to obtain food and locate reproduction sites. Different species possess various body features including claws, legs, wings, webbed feet, or fins to provide mobility. Jellyfish and squids move about using unique jet propulsion methods. Movement results after forcefully squirting water away from their bodies. In addition to adaptations for movement, some animals have specialized anatomical features that help them gather food. Birds are endowed with different types of beaks depending on their diets. Hawks have hooked, sharp beaks to tear small prey animals. Woodpeckers use long, pointed bills to drill into plants to find insects. Mosquitoes have needle-like mouths for sucking blood while grasshoppers have cutting jaws for chewing plants.

Squirrels, although having small brains, demonstrate excellent memory abilities. They are able to locate acorns or other food items buried previously. This species has learned that the location of perishable items must be accomplished over a relatively short period of time or their food stores will spoil. Squirrels have a memory of not only the location of each item, but also the time at which it should be eaten, indicating that they keep an inner record of food locations.

Reproductive strategies vary greatly among animals. Most reproduce through sexual activity between males and females. Thereafter, they may produce live births or lay fertilized eggs. Many sea animals reproduce through external fertilization. The female lays numerous egg cells and a male visits the site at a later time to release millions of sperm over the egg masses. Certain worms reproduce by releasing a portion of their bodies which consequently grows into a new animal.

Salmon and other similar fish spawn annually due to a change in photoperiod. They pursue dangerous and tiring journeys from the oceans where they live to return to streams where they were born originally. The female fish digs a pit in the gravel beneath a stream and deposits hundreds of eggs, after which a male comes along and fertilizes them. The spawning migration generally occurs during the fall, allowing the young to emerge from the gravel in springtime when the environment and food supplies are suitable for survival.

A unique phenomenon in several animal species is the production of pheromones. Pheromones are substances that are secreted or excreted by an animal that cause a specific reaction in another animal of the same species. The queen honeybee resides among a hive-full of worker bees. The workers are attracted by a pheromone released by the queen. This reaction allows the hive to stay and work together to produce honey. Numerous pheromones have been described as being active in various other insects. It is usually the female insect that releases the pheromone to attract mates. Commercially, synthetic pheromones have been developed to attract insects for extermination. Many mammals also produce pheromones which they deposit around their living areas or territories. These signals inform other animals of the same species to avoid invading an already inhabited territory.

Migration is common in many animals, frequently precipitated and regulated by magnetic influences from the moon and sun. These habitat changes by animals enable them to find satisfactory breeding and nesting sites, lay and incubate eggs, raise their young, locate better feeding areas, and avoid frigid temperatures. Birds can tell both times and dates, allowing species like garden warblers to migrate south in the winter by using the stars to navigate, but these signs provide only spatial dimensions. Warblers also need directional cues so they can determine when to fly south, how far they should travel, how long they should stay, and when to return back to their northern breeding sites. Should they make a mistake and fly either direction too early or late, or fly the wrong distances, they would miss other warblers and the chance for good feeding sites or the protection available through numbers during their trips. Further, a warbler who miscalculates timing for the journey north would miss finding good nesting sites and the best mates.

Humpback and blue whales migrate by traveling long distances from polar regions to waters near the equator that are warm for giving birth and raising their young. Bison know when they should migrate after being alerted by internal biological clocks, activated by changes in photoperiods. Their internal clocks tell them when to begin their migration journeys and the routes they should take without any additional directions.

Many species of animals hibernate which involves entering an inactive state caused by short daylight periods, cold temperatures, and limited food. Hibernating animals store food in their bodies so they can survive until warmer weather arrives when they can again find food. During hibernation, body functions are minimized and heart beats may be reduced to once or twice a minute. Bears, amphibians, reptiles, fish, bats, and insects all hibernate when living in areas where temperatures drop to low levels. Several of these smaller species burrow into the ground while bats and bears hibernate in caves or other enclosed areas. During cold seasons, rabbits, raccoons, and squirrels do not hibernate but spend considerable time sleeping in their burrows or nests. They emerge periodically on warm days to access the stores of food they accumulated previously.

God designed amazing protective anatomical features into the bodies of several animals and man. Many important or necessary organs were placed either under bony coverings, such as the cranium or rib cage, or they were created in pairs. Organs surrounded with bone are the brain, heart, pituitary gland, spleen, liver, and lungs. Those provided in pairs include the parathyroid glands, lungs, kidneys, adrenal glands, ovaries, and testes. Thus, if one of the paired organs fails or requires removal due to disease, the body can continue to function quite well with the single remaining organ.

God gave man dominion over the Earth. This includes providing care and protection for all animals. "Whoever is righteous has regard for the life of his beast, but the mercy of the wicked is cruel" (Proverbs 12:10). Special research programs and habitats have been established to isolate and breed endangered animal species. Zoos and animal parks also assist in protecting rare animals, ensuring their survival and reproduction. Further, rare or endangered plants are given protection throughout the world. Major programs involve diminishing soil erosion and maintaining fertile, productive soil. Additionally, worldwide environmental oversight is practiced constantly. Much is being done to protect the Earth and its inhabitants and more efforts should be initiated whenever deemed appropriate. God has given man a mandate to care for the Earth and its creatures and it behooves all mankind to nurture God's creation.

The pivotal question is, "How big is your God?" By Him, everything that exists was spoken into place in perfect sequential order. The sophisticated interactions among the created heavenly bodies, the Earth and its features, and plant and animal populations continue to operate flawlessly without failure. Evolution has never explained these marvels. Only an Almighty divine God could have accomplished these miraculous achievements. Our great God created!

"The Earth is the LORD'S and the fullness thereof, the world and those who dwell therein" (Psalm 24:1).

Chapter 9

Creation's Sequential Significance

"Worthy are you, our Lord and God, to receive glory and honor and power, for you created all things and by your will they existed and were created" (Revelation 4:11).

What less would one expect from a great God than a magnificent and massive creation fashioned to function in a precise, workable order? Starting with nothing and ending with man was no small feat. God prepared the universe for man and his dominion over all He created. This entire creation process was accomplished with an organized sequential plan that would allow perfect inclusion of each creative event at the optimum time. From the beginning, God has always had a perfect plan and He will continue to oversee and direct His divine oversight of the universe until the end of time.

Had He desired, God was surely capable of creating the entire universe and its inhabitants in an instant. Instead, He elected to use six 24-hour days ending on day seven with a day of rest. From the start, God knew what He wanted to accomplish and provided a specific day for man to worship Him as well as leaving time for rest and special activities.

On the first day of creation, the triune God spoke and formed an enormous dark, chaotic mass of mud, rocks, and water. Nothing is said in scripture about a big bang, a gap, nor long-term evolutionary refinements, primarily because none of these mythical events occurred.

This initial unorganized mass was not exactly a wonderful environment for anything. But, God had just begun and order was promptly on the way. After making this seemingly useless glob of material, He immediately dispensed the darkness. How exciting to realize that the sun would not appear until later but God Himself was the source of this original illumination. God is still in the business of introducing light and eliminating darkness from the souls of men! Certainly, God could have continued His creative work without light until creation of the sun on day four. So, why did He illuminate the universe on the first day? The answer to this question is unknown but God may have wanted future man to realize the importance of revealing his life-giving light early in creation, or He may have wished to see what he was creating over the next days.

On day one, God continued His creative work and fashioned the Earth with its various components: fertile soil, fuel resources, gems, minerals, rocks, and chemicals. Also included were gravitational forces that would prevent future created objects and beings from floating freely throughout the atmosphere. Additionally, magnetic fields were established to guide migration of future animals. Interestingly, the Earth was the first planet formed, likely because this would be the future home for man. Here is where God would send His only beloved Son to live among men and die as payment for their sins. And one glorious day, this is where God's Son, Jesus Christ, will return to rapture his redeemed children.

Having the Earth in order, God next created the heavens. The Third Heaven is still a mystery but we do know that this is the area where angels reside and redeemed individuals will spend eternity. Only an all-knowing God would have thought of this eventual need for His own children. The Second Heaven is the outer space expanse high above the Earth. New information about this area is gathered continually through space exploration flights. The space observed immediately above the Earth is the First Heaven which would become the atmosphere the following day.

The heavens, Earth, and light were created and God saw that they were good. He was now ready for day two of creation. A wonderful

Earth had been formed but there was water everywhere. On this second creative day, His flawless sequence continued by creating the firmament or atmosphere. Water resources located both above and on the Earth were separated. It is believed that the water placed above the Earth was actually a heavy vapor. This vapor would filter harmful rays from the future sun and prevent frigid temperatures in outer space from reaching the Earth, thus helping regulate climatic conditions. The vapor would also provide humidity needed for future plant life.

Sophisticated separate layers were created in the atmosphere consisting of the troposphere, stratosphere, mesosphere, and thermosphere. Each layer was designed to provide different needs for specific purposes. Among these atmospheric layers, vast stores of oxygen and nitrogen were added to sustain future plant, animal, and human life. Moisture was included to produce future humidity and rain. Also, atmospheric strata allowed water and chemicals to be recycled and permitted regulation of magnetic fields to govern climate control. Although much of the atmosphere is not seen, great benefits are provided by this vast area surrounding the Earth. On day two, the firmament was completed and the Earth was ready for dry land, seas, and vegetation.

On day three of creation God decided to address the soggy conditions on the Earth. He separated the water from the Earth and directed it into oceans, lakes, rivers, streams and ponds. The oceans were infused with a combination of oxygen and nitrogen to support eventual aquatic life. Continental shelves along ocean beaches were filled with sand, gravel, minerals, and petroleum reserves for later use by man. Evaporation from the surfaces of the numerous bodies of water entered the atmosphere for production of rain. This evaporative process also helped cool the water to provide appropriate temperatures for sea life.

Having confined the water, the Earth was now dry and could sustain plant life. Abundant varieties of numerous plants, consisting of grasses, crops, vegetables, flowers, shrubs, and trees, were spoken into existence. The various soil types and nutritional ingredients required for the multiplicity of different plants were already available from the first day of creation. Plant structures such as leaves, flowers, fruits, roots, stems, and trunks were appropriately modified for each environmental locale. Desert plants were designed to withstand hot, dry temperatures while others were fashioned for wet, cool, sunny, or shady conditions. Such miracles would hardly have sprung from a prolonged evolutionary process!

A great variety of useful plant products was available for the arrival of animals and man. Since animals and man were originally vegetarians, plant food items were of considerable value. These included fruits, roots, tubers, bulbs, pods, leaves, seeds, and syrup. Myriad flowers provided beauty and also some types of food. Medicinal products would eventually be found in many of the created plants. Other useful purposes of plants would include the processing of pigments and oils, production of fibers for clothing, and the use of wood for building materials or fuel.

A unique characteristic of plants is their ability to use carbon dioxide and emit oxygen; exactly the opposite from that found in animals and man. Could evolution have developed such an efficient system? Day three of creation set the stage for future living inhabitants. There were now bodies of water for aquatic animals, voluminous quantities of plants for food and useful resources, trees for nesting animals, and methods for production of rain and climate control.

All plants created on day three needed an energy source, different seasons, and day-night cycles for continued growth and replication. On day four, God created the sun which energized photosensitization in plants, allowing them to manufacture food. The sun also provided heat to stimulate seed germination and plant development. On this same day, God created the moon, stars, seasons, days, and years. In addition, billions of other stars and planets in the universe were created on day four.

Movements of the planets caused the different seasons, days, and years. Seasons were defined by nearness of the Earth to the sun as this planet rotated on a tilted axis. Days were established by 24-hour rotations of the Earth. Years were measured by the Earth's annual orbits around the sun. Gravitational forces, which were created within the sun and moon, caused tidal waves in the Earth's oceans. These waves would aid in distribution of aquatic plants and animals and govern feeding and reproduction activities in marine animals.

Daily light and dark cycles governed hormonal interactions which regulated reproduction in animals and man. Further, these cycles facilitate breeding and feeding in nocturnal animals. Nights permitted plants, animals, and man to rest and become revitalized for the next day's activities. With the vast creation of the thousands of heavenly bodies, day four was, indeed, significant.

The Earth was now well-organized with its energy sources and abundant food supplies. The next creative event in a sensible sequence would be the appearance of animals. On day five, God created sea animals, birds, and insects. God again exhibited His greatness by creating thousands of varieties of these animals, each suited for a specific environment. Space for this multitude of animals was not a problem since some lived in the open spaces above the Earth, others in the bodies of water, and the remainder either on or within the Earth.

Previous creative events provided the needs for these animals. Changes in day length and light intensity (photoperiods) triggered molting in birds during which they renewed their feathers. Altering photoperiods also enhanced production of offspring and singing in pet birds as well as increased egg laying in domestic fowl. Magnetic fields directed migration in several animal species and calibrated internal clocks in bees to navigate them toward specific areas. A large array of insects assisted in pollinating plants, provided food for birds and fish, and processed dead plants or animals into soil-enriching material.

The Earth was teeming with life; however, the animals were not to be consumed as food by other animals or man until after the Noahic flood. On day six God made livestock, beasts, creeping things and, finally, His ultimate creation, man. Initially, livestock or the common farm animals would supply man with milk and eggs. Changing photoperiods resulted in higher milk production from dairy cows, and earlier breeding patterns and improved hair growth in horses. Many of the created animals provided companionship, clothing, transportation, protection, entertainment, and sport, plus several species performed work. The wild and creeping animals were very interesting, especially as they demonstrated God's handiwork and even His sense of humor on occasion. Their habits and behaviors were designed to bring joy to mankind.

God's final creation was man. He created man in His image and He wants to be involved in fellowship and worship with Him. During His entire creative process God only said once, after day six, that what He had made was very good. Man is a special creation that was fearfully and wonderfully made. "For you formed my inward parts; you knitted me together in my mother's womb. I praise you, for I am fearfully and wonderfully made" (Psalm 139:13-14). Human structures, functions, and emotions are different from those found in animals, a fact generally ignored by ardent evolutionists. God entrusted man to have dominion over His creation, a high honor and great responsibility. Therefore, it behooves man to be a good steward of all God has given him.

After completing the entire universe, creation ceased and God proclaimed a day of rest. Although He did not give detailed directions for man's activities on the weekly day of rest, He did provide some guidance. Certainly, man is to have fellowship with God and other Christians and he is commanded to worship God. Additionally, from His instructions, it can be assumed that only necessary work should be done and the day should be kept holy.

The sensible sequence of creation is undeniable. God made the Earth and provided everything man would need. In addition, there are still numerous unknown aspects of creation that will likely continue to benefit man. He made the sun to energize the growth of plants and, then, He created all kinds of animal species. God made plants to provide food for man initially and the animals were given for food following the Noahic flood. All the food, gems, fuel resources, minerals, wood, and other building materials were provided at precise times to harmonize with each succeeding creative event. It would be impossible for anyone but God to have planned everything to work together in such a superb way. Evolution would never have accomplished this extraordinary feat.

God loved man and He personally planted a beautiful garden for him. Sadly, man failed God and sinned; he would not live forever but was condemned to die. Thereafter, a most gracious God sent His only Son to die on a cruel cross for man's sins. God had spent six days creating everything for man but he rebelled. Could it be that God's gracious creative plan, beginning with a chaotic mass and ending with His ultimate creation, man, may have grieved His heart?

Indeed, God created the massive universe in a magnificent and orderly manner. His creative plan was accomplished in perfect sequential order. And He still maintains and operates the entire universe, providing a home for man. After man's failure, God still loves him and wants to redeem him for His own. If you are not His child, please read the next chapter, "Does it Really Matter?"

"Thus the heavens and the Earth were finished, and all the hosts of them" (Genesis 2:1).

Chapter 10

Does It Really Matter?

"For God so loved the world, that he gave his only Son, that whoever believes in him should not perish but have eternal life" (John 3:16).

The Bible authenticates that God created the entire universe and its inhabitants in six literal 24-hour days. What scripture reveals about creation has never been disproven but, rather, has been and continues to be verified repeatedly. Sadly, the theory of evolution has been unable to provide a single plausible answer, but simply confuses the phenomenal events that occurred during the week of divine creation. Indeed, God created!

In the beginning, on the first day of creation, God produced light. This light did not come from the sun but was cosmic illumination from God himself. From the start, He was the light that would be available to illuminate men's hearts and redeem their souls. The following scriptural references describe God's life-giving light. "The LORD is my light and my salvation; whom shall I fear? The LORD is the stronghold of my life; of whom shall I be afraid?" (Psalm 27:1). "Again Jesus spoke to them, saying, I am the light of the world. Whoever follows me will not walk in darkness, but will have the light of life" (John 8:12).

Previous chapters have presented the entire creation record in some detail. As expansive as these acts were, God wants each reader to experience His new creation. The same divine God who created man initially also conceived his second or new creation. "Therefore, if anyone is in Christ, he is a new creation" (2 Corinthians 5:17). Once man sinned in the Garden of Eden, God said that he would die forfeiting his right to live forever. In order to receive eternal life, man had to be reborn. "Jesus answered him, Truly, truly, I say to you, unless one is born again he cannot see the kingdom of God" (John 3:3). Even though man fell from grace, he had great value to God. God cared about the life of one of His smaller creations, the sparrow, and extends special grace for the redemption of His ultimate creation, man. "Are not two sparrows sold for a penny? And not one of them will fall to the ground apart from your Father" (Matthew 10:29). For man to come back into God's favor, the eternal God, who spoke the universe into being, devised a plan for man's redemption. He lovingly sent His Son down from heaven to die on a cruel and shameful cross to give man a second chance for eternal life.

Life's most important question is, "Where are you going when you die?" How good one has been, how nice you treat others, whether or not you have been baptized or are a church member, or how much you give to the poor or charity has nothing to do with salvation. God gives this gift freely and wholly through his grace. "For by grace you have been saved through faith. And this is not your own doing; it is the gift of God, not a result of works, so that no one may boast" (Ephesians 2:8-9).

The free gift of salvation, or eternal life, is presented clearly in the Bible. To be born again, you must first admit you are a sinner. "For all have sinned and fall short of the glory of God, and are justified by his grace as a gift, through the redemption that is in Christ Jesus" (Romans 3:23-24). Because of our sin, we are condemned to death. "For the wages of sin is death" (Romans 6:23). This death means eternal separation from God forever.

Now comes the good part for everyone who has sinned and lost the guarantee of eternal life. God loved every human being so much that He sacrificed His only begotten Son, Jesus, on a cross to pay for our sins and die in our place. "But God shows his love for us in that while we were still sinners, Christ died for us" (Romans 5:8). Although, impossible for the human mind to comprehend such love, Jesus took our load of sin as our substitute.

The Bible teaches that we must believe in Jesus who took our sins and died for us. Jesus was crucified, buried, and resurrected, and resides in heaven with God. To be saved, one must call on Jesus as Lord and Savior. "For everyone who calls on the name of the Lord will be saved" (Romans 10:13). If you are ready to receive Christ as your Savior, it is necessary for you to ask Him to forgive your sins and commit your life fully to Him. "Because, if you confess with your mouth that Jesus is Lord and believe in your heart that God raised him from the dead, you will be saved. For with the heart one believes and is justified, and with the mouth one confesses and is saved." (Romans 10:9-10). Following is an appropriate prayer you may wish to recite asking Jesus for salvation from all your sins:

"Father, I know that I am a sinner and that I am separated from You. I am sorry for my sins and want to turn my life over to You. I ask for your forgiveness believing that your Son, Jesus Christ died for my sins, was resurrected from the dead, is alive, and hears me right now. I invite Jesus to reign in my heart and life from this day forward. Thank you for the help of your Holy Spirit to enable me to live for you and help me tell others about their need for salvation. In Jesus' name I pray. Amen."

If you have prayed this prayer sincerely, you are now a child of God. The journey from your original creation to a new creation is complete. You have been born again and will spend eternity in the eternal city of heaven after you die. Your salvation or new creation is the most important decision to be made while living on earth. It really does matter. Praise God for his wonderful creations!

"And the city has no need of sun or moon to shine on it, for the glory of God gives it light, and its lamp is the Lamb"
(Revelation 21:23).

Selected Readings

Attenborough, D. *The Life of Mammals*. Princeton University Press, Princeton, NJ, 2002.

Brewer, S. *1,001 Facts about the Human Body*. Dorling Kindersley, New York, NY, 2002.

Caprara, G. *The Solar System*. Firefly Books, Buffalo, NY, 2003.

Cogger, H.G., and Zweifel, R.G. (Eds). *Encyclopedia of Reptiles and Amphibians*. Academic Press, San Diego, CA, 1998.

Folkens, P.A., Reeves, R.R., Stewart, B.S., Clapham, P.J., and Powell, J.A. *Guide to Marine Mammals of the World*. Alfred A. Knopf, Inc., New York, NY, 2002.

Foster, R.G., and Kreitzman, L. *Rhythms of Life*. Yale University Press, New Haven, CT, 2004.

Hancock, P.L., and Skinner, B.J. (Eds). *The Oxford Companion to the Earth*. Oxford University Press, New York, NY, 2000.

Jonas, G. *North American Trees*. The Reader's Digest Association, Inc., Pleasantville, NY, 1993.

McNab, D., and Jounger. J. *The Planets*. Yale University Press, New Haven, CT, 1999.

Morris, H.M. *The Genesis Record*. Baker Book House, Grand Rapids, MI, 1976.

Prager, E.J., and Earle, S.A. *The Oceans*. McGraw-Hill, New York, NY, 2000.

Preston-Mafham, R., and Preston-Mafham, K. *The Natural History of Insects*. The Crowood Press, Wiltshire, England, 1996.

Ridpath, I. (Ed). *The Illustrated Encyclopedia of the Universe*. Watson-Guptill Publications, New York, NY, 2001.

Thibodeau, G.A., and Patton, K.T. *Structure & Function of the Body*. Mosby, Inc., St. Louis, MO, 2000.

Wade, N. (Ed.) *The Science Times Book of Birds*. The Lyons Press, New York, NY, 1997.

Whitfield, P. (Ed). *The Simon and Schuster Encyclopedia of Animals*. Simon and Schuster Editions, New York, NY, 1998.